MORE RYAN'S WORLD OF SCIENCE

Ready-to-Read

Simon Spotlight
New York   London   Toronto   Sydney   New Delhi

While the following experiments don't pose any significant safety hazards, all activities should have proper safety precautions and adult supervision.

SIMON SPOTLIGHT
An imprint of Simon & Schuster Children's Publishing Division
1230 Avenue of the Americas, New York, New York 10020
This Simon Spotlight edition June 2021
Text by Aubre Andrus
TM & © 2021 RTR Production, LLC, RFR Entertainment, Inc. and Remka, Inc., and PocketWatch, Inc. Ryan ToysReview, Ryan's World and all related titles, logos and characters are trademarks of RTR Production, LLC, RFR Entertainment, Inc. and Remka, Inc. The pocket.watch logo and all related titles, logos and characters are trademarks of PocketWatch, Inc. All Rights Reserved. Photos and illustrations of Ryan and Ryan's World characters copyright © 2021 RTR Production, LLC, RFR Entertainment, Inc. and Remka, Inc. • Stock photos and illustrations by iStock
All rights reserved, including the right of reproduction in whole or in part in any form. SIMON SPOTLIGHT, READY-TO-READ, and colophon are registered trademarks of Simon & Schuster, Inc.
For more information about special discounts for bulk purchases, please contact Simon & Schuster Special Sales at 1-866-506-1949 or business@simonandschuster.com.
Manufactured in the United States of America 0521 LAK
2 4 6 8 10 9 7 5 3 1
ISBN 978-1-5344-8532-7 (hc)
ISBN 978-1-5344-8531-0 (pbk)
ISBN 978-1-5344-8533-4 (eBook)

Hi, I am Ryan! Today I am doing science experiments. Come along with me!

EXPERIMENT: RAINING CLOUDS

Why does it rain?

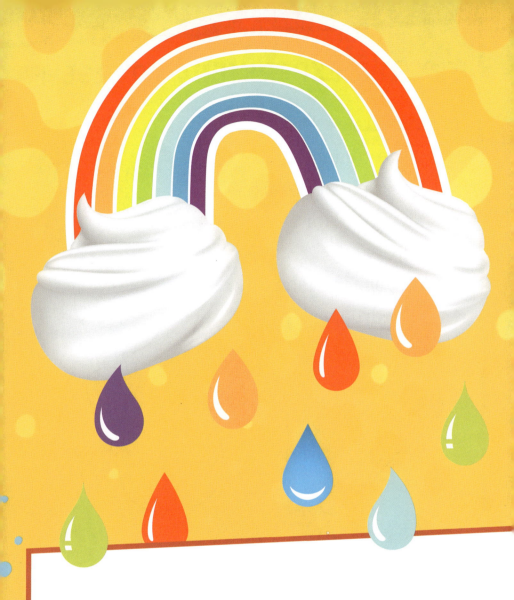

We will use
shaving cream
and colored water
to find out!

TRY THE EXPERIMENT YOURSELF!

YOU WILL NEED:
- 1 large container, like a water pitcher or fishbowl
- shaving cream
- 1 cup
- food coloring (any color is fine)
- an eyedropper

Always do the experiment with a grown-up.

1. Fill the large container with water until it is mostly full.

2. Squirt a layer of shaving cream on top of the water.

3. Fill the cup with water. Add two drops of food coloring and stir.

4. Fill the eyedropper with the colored water.

5. Release a drop of the colored water into the shaving cream. Add more drops. Watch what happens!

Use as many different colors of food coloring as you would like.

A cloud is made up of many drops of water.

The drops of water join together to make bigger drops.
When the drops of water get too heavy, they fall. This is called rain.

In the experiment, the colored drops get heavier inside the cloud of shaving cream.

Then they fall into the water below. It is just like rain!

EXPERIMENT: CAN YOU COOK WITH THE SUN?

Now it is sunny, and I am hungry.

I wonder if we can cook using heat from the sun. Do you want to try?

TRY THE EXPERIMENT YOURSELF!

First, you will make an oven.

Always do the experiment with a grown-up.

You will need:
- 1 pizza box
- plastic wrap
- aluminum foil
- black paper
- a ruler
- scissors
- tape

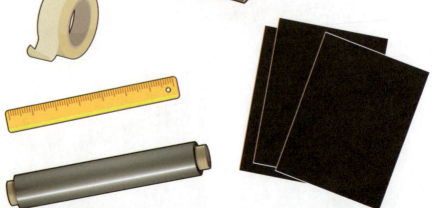

1. Ask a grown-up to cut a square flap into the lid of the pizza box. Make sure to leave at least two inches between the square and the edges of the lid.

2. Fold the flap up. Cover the inside of the flap with aluminum foil. Tape down the foil to hold it in place.

3. Open the box lid. Place black paper in the bottom of the box.

4. Cover the square window on the lid by taping plastic wrap over it.

Now you will cook a sweet s'more!

You will need:
- 2 graham crackers
- 1 marshmallow
- 1 piece of chocolate

Always do the experiment with a grown-up.

1. Open the box. Place the graham crackers on the black paper.
2. Put the marshmallow on top of one graham cracker. Put the chocolate on top of the other cracker.
3. Close the box and put it outside in direct sunlight.

4. Lift the flap. Use a ruler to keep it propped up.
5. Check on the s'more about once every fifteen minutes.
6. Remove the food from the box when the chocolate and marshmallow are melted.
7. Stack the crackers together like a sandwich. Now your s'more is ready to eat!

The sunnier it is, the faster your s'more will be ready!

How does the oven cook the s'more? It uses solar power, which is energy gathered from the sun.

The rays of sunshine shine onto the flap. The foil points the rays into the box.

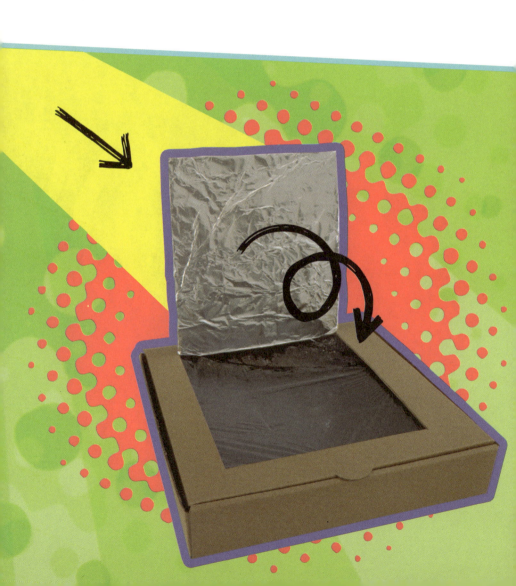

The plastic wrap traps the heat of the rays. The black paper soaks it in.

The heat melts the chocolate and the marshmallow. Solar power is cool . . . I mean, warm!

EXPERIMENT: HOMEMADE ICE CREAM

I used heat to make a treat. Now I will use ice to make another treat.

Did you know that you can make ice cream in a bag?
It is easy!

TRY THE EXPERIMENT YOURSELF!

YOU WILL NEED:
- 1/2 cup half-and-half
- 1/4 teaspoon vanilla extract
- 1 tablespoon sugar
- 1/3 cup salt
- 4 cups ice
- 1 medium zipper-top bag
- 1 large zipper-top bag

Always do the experiment with a grown-up.

1. Pour the half-and-half, vanilla, and sugar into the medium bag. Squeeze the air out of the bag and close it tightly.

2. Fill one third of the large bag with ice. Add the salt.

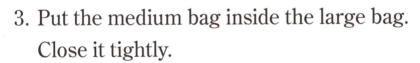

3. Put the medium bag inside the large bag. Close it tightly.

4. Shake the large bag carefully until the ice cream starts to form inside the medium bag. It will take about five to ten minutes.
5. Remove the medium bag from the large bag. Scoop the ice cream into a bowl. Yum!

How does the cream in the medium bag turn into ice cream?

Salt helps ice melt more easily. But ice also needs heat to melt.

The ice uses heat from the cream to melt. This makes the cream get colder and colder . . . until it turns into ice cream!

Shaking also helps the cream freeze faster. Science is so fun, and it tastes yummy!

Thank you for joining me today.

I hope you like science as much as I do!

Dear parents and caregivers,

I'm Loann, Ryan's mom. I used to be a science teacher, so I know that science experiments are very important for getting children excited about learning. Science isn't just something that happens in a book or a YouTube video. It's also something that your child can observe in real life. Ryan loves it when he can see, smell, touch, and hear science—and sometimes taste it too!

You might think that science experiments require a lot of setup and cleanup. Don't worry! The experiments in this book are specially designed to be simple and easy to do at home. Ryan and I love experimenting together and learning new things along the way.

I hope these science experiments will help grow your child's interest in science. As Ryan always says: science is COOL!

—Loann